LOOK MOMMY

I CAN READ THIS WORD!

Vol. 2

Margaret B. Lovick, M.Ed.

TABLE OF CONTENTS

Sight Words with Short 'E' Sound

Bed

(write the sight word in the sentence)

I love to read on my______.

Beg

(write the sight word in the sentence)

My dog always ____ me to play with him.

Bet

(write the sight word in the sentence)

I ____ he will make this basketball shot.

Den

(write the sight word in the sentence)

The bears are in the ______.

Fed

(write the sight word in the sentence)

Mom ____ us pizza for dinner.

5

Gel

(write the sight word in the sentence)

I put ____ in my hair every day.

Get

(write the sight word in the sentence)

The doorbell is ringing, ____ the door!

Hen

(write the sight word in the sentence)

The ___ and her baby are on a farm.

Jet

(write the sight word in the sentence)

Wow! A big _____ is landing.

Led

(write the sight word in the sentence)

He ___the marching band in the parade.

Leg

(write the sight word in the sentence)

The little boy hurt his ___.

Let

It's raining, please ____ me in!

Men

The ___ are building a house.

Met

I ____ a new friend at school.

Net

(write the sight word in the sentence)

I caught a butterfly in my ___.

Peg

(write the sight word in the sentence)

I put my jacket on the ___ in my room.

Pen

I wrote Santa a letter with a black ____.

Pet

(write the sight word in the sentence)

I love my ____ goldfish.

Red

(write the sight word in the sentence)

My _____ car is my favorite toy.

Ref

(write the sight word in the sentence)

The ____ blew the whistle to stop the game.

20

Set

(write the sight word in the sentence)

My bear and I always play
with my tea ___.

21

Ten

(write the sight word in the sentence)

Today's my birthday,
I am ___ years old.

Vet

(write the sight word in the sentence)

The ___ takes care of all the animals.

Web

The spider is hanging from the ___.

Wet

(write the sight word in the sentence)

Oh, no! My dress is ____.

Great Job!

You have learned ...

Twenty-five (25) new sight words with the short " A" sound.

Learned how to write twenty-five (25) new sight words.

Learned how to spell twenty-five (25) new sight words.

Learned how to read the twenty-five (25) new sight words in a sentence.

Keep reading every day!

Your Friend...Teacher
Margaret B. Lovick, M.Ed.